To parents and teachers

Take this opportunity to help children devel[illegible] effective social behavior. Research has shown that socially competent children are more accepted in school by both teachers and peers AND have higher achievement.

Our goal here is to help children deal with feelings of anger. The suggestions that follow are to help you make the best use of this book.

Before you read

Look at the cover of the book. Derek's in the principal's office. Why do you think he is there?

Look at the title of the book. Why do you think he's in trouble? What do kids do in school that gets them sent to the office?

Imagine how Derek is feeling. How do you feel when you're in trouble?

Predict what you think Derek did to get into trouble. Let's find out together.

While you read

Continue to ask questions.

- p. 3: Have you figured out yet what Derek's problem is? Why is it a problem? What happens when you fight at school? When you're angry at someone, what else could you do besides fight?
- p. 7: What happens to Derek when he fights at school?
- p. 11: Did Derek have to hit Steven? What else could he have done?
- p. 15: What did the principal tell Derek to do when he was angry? What does your body feel like when you're angry? Why might you need time to "cool down"? What will taking deep breaths do for you? (Practice taking deep breaths while counting to ten.) List the things the principal told Derek to do. (1. Take 10 deep breaths. 2. Think about what you want to say. 3. Use a calm voice. 4. Or, decide to walk away.)
- p. 19: How did Derek feel when Jason tried to take his ball? What did Derek do? Why is this a better way to handle your anger?
- p. 21: How are you feeling when you clench your fists? What did Derek decide to do?
- p. 23: In the end, what did Derek learn?

After you read

Provide more examples of when Derek might get angry. Practice following the steps to control anger.

1. His best friend laughs at him.
2. Someone stole his pencil.
3. He lost a game of checkers with his brother.

Fill out the "story structure" below.

The problem in this story was	⇨	This was a problem because	⇨	The problem was finally solved when	⇨	In the end

Give sentence starters (i.e., for journal writing)

I feel angry or mad when....

When I am angry, I sometimes....

A better way to express my anger might be....

When I am angry, the people I could talk to are....

I'm always in trouble,
Always in a fight.
It's not my fault
Nothing goes right.

I have problems at home,
Problems at school.
How can I solve them
And still be cool?

HELPING
SHARING
JFN
92

Mom says I'm a wimp
If I don't fight.
Teacher says don't do it,
It's just not right.

What am I to do,
Caught in the middle?
School says don't fight,
Not even a little!

Now, when I'm mad
I want to fight.
I feel like hitting
The first kid in sight.

And when I do
I'm in lots of trouble.
"Off to the office,
On the double!"

OFFICE

Sitting in the office
Is not any fun.
I'd rather be outside
To play and run.

The principal asks,
"Why do you fight?
Fighting at school
Is just not right."

PRINCIPAL STERN.

Troubles follow me
Wherever I go.
I climb the bars
And wouldn't you know

The kid behind
Says I'm too slow.
"Get off the bars or
I'll grab your toe!"

That made me so mad.
I had to get even.
That's the reason
I had to hit Steven.

*“When you’re mad,
About to fight,
Control your anger with
All your might.*

*"Take deep breaths,
Count to ten,
Before you try
To talk again.*

1..2...3...
4...5...6..
7...8...9...
10!!

"Think about
What you want to say--
Or make a decision
To walk away.

"If you can't use
A cool, calm voice,
To walk away
Is a better choice."

My troubles didn't
Go away.
They followed me
Throughout the day.

When I got mad,
I did things right.
I went a whole day
Without a fight.

Jason tried
To take my ball.
I counted to ten,
Didn't yell at all.

Instead I said,
"Throw the ball to me.
Let's play soccer.
Bounce it off your knee."

**A kid called me a name.
It made me mad.
My fists were clenched.
It could be bad.**

**I counted to ten
In my head.
"Knock it off,"
Is all I said.**

1,2,3,4,
5,6,7,8,9,
...10!

Cool cats can
Keep their cool,
Even when they're
Mad at school.

Staying out of trouble
Is much more fun.
I play with friends,
Get more things done.

I won't miss the principal.
I won't miss the hall.
I won't miss detention.
They're no fun at all!

When you're mad,
About to fight,
Control your anger
With all your might!

Take deep breaths,
Count to ten,
Before you try
To talk again.

If you can't use
A cool, calm voice,
To walk away
Is a better choice.

(Permission is granted to enlarge this page for a wall chart.)